"Stark Naked is a brave, bare-to-the-bone journey into the dark by a powerful new voice in Australian poetry."

–Janeen Webb, a multiple-award-winning author, editor, critic and academic.

"Stark Naked is a powerful poetry collection, written by an author who does not pull punches. Silvia Canton Rondoni slices open her flesh, bares her soul, and dares us to take a look at the darkness inside. Raw, painful, and filled with emotion; her poems get under your skin and stay there. Highly recommended."

–Owl Goingback, Bram Stoker Award-Winning author of *Crota* and *Coyote Rage*.

"Silvia Canton Rondoni's chapbook Stark Naked is an astonishing marriage of poetry and graphic art, for Silvia Nieto's black and white illustrations serve to heighten and harmonize the anger, poignancy, and vulnerability captured by the poet's penetrating, crystal-edged verse."

–Jack Dann, Nebula, World Fantasy, Aurealis, and Shirley Jackson awards-winning author and editor.

"Silvia Cantón Rondoni has a real gift for expression. Reading this collection is an intimate experience, as delicate tissues of words form over the wounds left by hatred, fear and love. You are left wanting to hug those closest to you."

–Kyla Lee Ward, writer of speculative fiction, poet and actor, Aurealis Award winner.

"Interwoven with intense body imagery, Silvia Cantón Rondoni's bitingly honest 'Stark Naked' poetry collection invites us to 'plunge under her skin', feel her 'tentacles of fear', be 'infected by her bone-deep' grief and witness her struggles against regrets that are 'rocks inside her pockets'. Shunning the ghosts of lost loves, rising above physical disability, family cruelty, social exclusion and ethnic bias, Rondoni emerges triumphant to 'take pride in her scars'. Beautifully illustrated throughout by Silvia Nieto, this book is an uncompromising probing of personal trauma and deeply lived experience."

–Anne Casey, award-winning Sydney-based poet and writer.

IFWG Publishing Chapbooks

Black Moon (Eugen Bacon) 2020
Tool Tales (Kaaron Warren & Ellen Datlow) 2021
Stark Naked (Silvia Cantón Rondoni) 2021

An IFWG Publishing Chapbook

STARK NAKED

An Illustrated Poetry Collection

by Silvia Cantón Rondoni

Illustrated by Silvia Nieto

Stark Naked

All Rights Reserved

ISBN-13: 978-1-922556-10-3

Copyright ©2021 Silvia Cantón Rondoni

Cover art/design and internal art by Silvia Nieto

V1.0

IFWG Publishing International
www.ifwgpublishing.com

Gold Coast, Australia

I wish to thank each and every one of those who let me down,
to those passers-by that came around and were soon gone
and especially to the brutes that took me down.

Without you I'd be nothing more
than a privileged, entitled little cunt.

Adversity brought me resilience, perspective and drive,
time and patience made me realise who was there in the long run.

To my parents, Montse, Felix, Xisca and Juan.
To my soul family, Silvia and Chris.

To the Brown-Coughlan family for taking me in.
To Gerry, for his guidance.
To Paul, *aroha nui*.

DISCLAIMER

Stark naked
serene
I let you in.
Plunge
under my skin
get to know
who I've been.
Take a deep breath
unearth
who I was
diving bone deep.
Judge if you will
my now, my then
my naïveté
for I take pride
in the scars I bear.
Anger, grief, love
tore me apart.
Persistence, hope, grit
ensconced within.
This collection
of poems
unfold the story
of who I want to be.

THEN

Broken,
cocooned and forgotten.
Out of touch, yet breathing.
Numb, kept going, like never before.

But it's the wrong place
and it's the wrong time.
My spirit crushing under reality,
a pain that can't be subdued.

Hands on my tools, I am ready.
The time has come to dig a deeper hole.
Give it all up. Put yourself to blame.
But hold on, is it really?

For I can chose to take it all in,
love, sorrow, pain and grief.
Allow intensity to break through
all of my defences,
for there is nothing to control
when you're nothing at all.

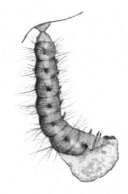

Now

Elevated.
Free and wild.
Transcendent and calm.
Perspective bringing purpose
to flesh, mind and soul.

Present. Steady.
Aware, yet observant.
At peace with my surroundings.

Timeless. Alive.
Unlimited and full of warmth.
A collector of precious moments.

Ink filing pages
of the books that could still be.
If only I dare
to get myself out there. Once more.

Feel it all. Give in.
Discard what's dispensable.
Concern yourself not,
everything will flow.
Liquid poetry.
Glow.

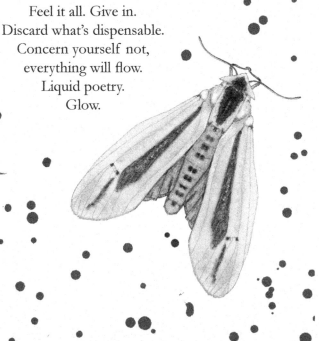

UNDER MY SKIN

IF ONLY I KNEW

If only I knew
I'd feel so grounded
standing up by myself.
I'd not have wasted my youth
chasing dreams
that weren't mine
to begin with.
Nothing but mere ideals
where I should be
how I must get there.
Instead of seeking for
the one and only
I could have seen her/me
staring back in the mirror
in highs and lows.

If only I knew
that love will bring grief
and from loss
will rise the anger
that will set
my words on fire.
I'd have not given up
all I was
to move to Australia.
Yet I don't regret a thing
for I fully lived,
it took me some time to learn
that if only I knew
I'd do it all over again.

ORIGINS

I came from unskilled,
unschooled blue-collar offspring.
A projected success
of the oppressed.
Forced to believe
in what I could be,
and because of it
unable to submit.

A ne'er-do-well,
awkward try-hard
daring like no one else
to excel.
Flying towards the sun
unrealistic expectations
melted wings mid-flight.

Strange lands, one after another,
taught me I'd never
be tough enough.
Infected wounds
set me back yet didn't stop me.

A pretender
that's who they see in me
doomed to fail as ever
no matter what.
A rebel
that's who I am,
cursed to keep trying
until the end of time.

A creative mind
that's who I remain
held onto savaged flesh
by a thin thread.
Not longing
to fit in with those unable to rise
not to join the star-struck wise.

Leave me where I roam
my part time life, my full-time quest
to unearth others like me.
Uninhibited spirits, wild mavericks
withstand despair and do not concede
for we are free. To be.

NOBODY. SOMEBODY

nobody
has ever known me
the way I do

nobody
has ever touched me
the way I can

nobody
has ever loved me
the way I have

nobody
understands
I want not
what I have
nor what I need
but what I deserve

somebody
that takes the time
to know me

somebody
that learns just how
to hold me

somebody
that can't help but
to love me

I DARE YOU TO LOVE ME

I dare you to love me
find my eyes and hold it
until your heart skips a beat
adrenaline rushing
within

Inspired, you can finally see
the measure
of who you have been
and the magnitude
of who you could be.

I dare you to love me
lay by my side and read me
stories birthed from your fears
echoes from a past long gone
turned into the present you own.

Intimidated, you start to comprehend
you can't have what you most crave.

Hence my dare
to push yourself
far beyond your dreams
to love yourself as you do me.

Show up unannounced
make a scene
prove you are worthy
of me.

SUDDEN REALISATION

I've no path here
frustration ignited from my otherness.
I've no work here
thrown from a career I once shone in.
I've no choice clear
but to reinvent myself, move on.

This empty life of mine,
this man I've chosen to be with
this house of ours, these rooms
blank canvases filled with neglect
a place we never made our own.

We lost the way,
stranded were you and
trusting your lead,
I (we) failed to see
the void closing in.

You fell and I hesitated
watching from above
unable to help
too late for what it was worth.

Rock bottom you reached
and looking up
call me out for me to join
throwing myself into the unknown.

But I could not
and I will not,
triggers peaked
for I've been there
in another life, long gone.

Let it be fear
writing horror stories, finding my tribe
conventions keeping me away
from what I know how to fix not.

Let it be what it may
frozen in place
watching every move
holding onto swords
I don't wish to sway.

Let it be me
content on my own
no longer seeking love
ready to comprehend
that I must be alone.

Just as the first light of dawn blinds me
I glimpse the future to come
everything I could ever have
if I no longer freeze
nor fight, but flee.

AWAKENING

You took my hand
as if it was yours not mine
and my heart followed.
We attained the other
on a crisp London eve
wanted to be seen
lust rushing us in.
A deal was made
a discreet embrace of the soul
was all we could take
and all we could give.

Months ran by since
craving a repeat
of what will never be.
Scenes unfolding
fingers reaching out within
succumbing
hoping you'll feel
across the seas
as inclined as I am
to put yourself together
no longer pretending to live
deprived.

Unobtainable, uncontainable, untraceable feat
unsustainable, uncontrollable plead
dispossessed of what little sense
I ever had, lost, mislead, grieving
on a crisp London eve.

Dear Chris

You were never mine
to hold onto, to let you go.
Your soul fastened to mine
warm sun on a late summer day
unexpected bliss I never earned.
You are gone yet I feel you
roaming spaces in between
whispering words in my ear
stretched tentacles seizing
each and every one of my fears.
I am blessed to have ever met you
grateful for our conversations
for the long sleepless nights we had
our constant source of inspiration.

Grief is finally letting go of me
no longer angry, nor wishing for the universe
to burst into flames just to ease my pain.
The things we shared will never fade
my craving for life will never cease
keeping on writing, drawing, for you, for me.
For everyone whose ever lost
the most precious connection
do not fear, we are all here.
Building a new path ahead
to honour those no longer among us
to spread the love we once felt
to find the words to express:
You are and will always be my inspiration
your life was not in vain.

BONE DEEP

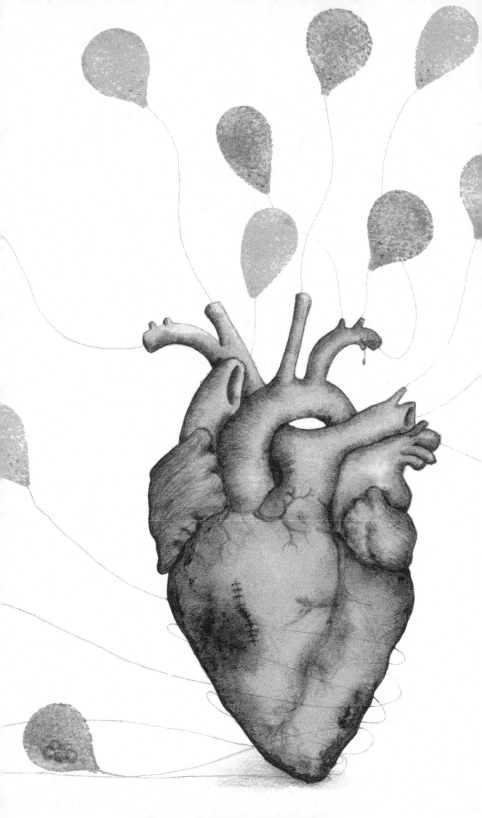

INFECTIOUS SORROW

The idea is
that when you lose
a loved one
in a sudden, painful way,
you must write down
something you wish
you had the chance to say
when they're near
so it can be released back
to their spirit wherever they may be.
When you are done,
insert your message into a balloon's haul
and hold it until you're ready to release.

I filled the study with them.
Balloons
every colour of the rainbow
piling up to the roof
until I could fit no more.
Just that room
for that's where I had been
when you went missing
when I watched them looking
when they found you
floating in the harbour
just like them.
Balloons.

Taking up space
filled with my sorrows
the things I could've said
the things I could've done
are rocks inside my pockets
carrying me down
into the deepest pit
where no one can find me.

The idea is
to learn to let go
but I know I never will.
The dark places we inhabit
hold your light no more
but somehow I feel I do.
Every memory
every melody
every gift sent and done
matches what gave me light and warmth
in the lonely night of the soul.
Learning to let go
of how others think I should grieve
of how others feel I should move on
finding my own way
to celebrate
having you in life
even if for a short time
until we meet again.

BUZZED UP.
POST-CON DISORDER

Atoms excited
buzz around us
when writers collide.
Storytellers, poets,
born scribes,
from every corner
worldwide.
My tribe, my fam,
whānau, mi gente.
Not enough conventions
to meet everyone
not enough chances
to hold onto this flow.
We lift each other up
here, there, everywhere.

I never dreamt
to belong like I do
creative master-minds
having my back
supporting each other
just like that.
All writers, unite
aspiring, emerging, established
we can do this.
What was once
the most solitary craft
is not so no more
for I know you are
standing by my side.

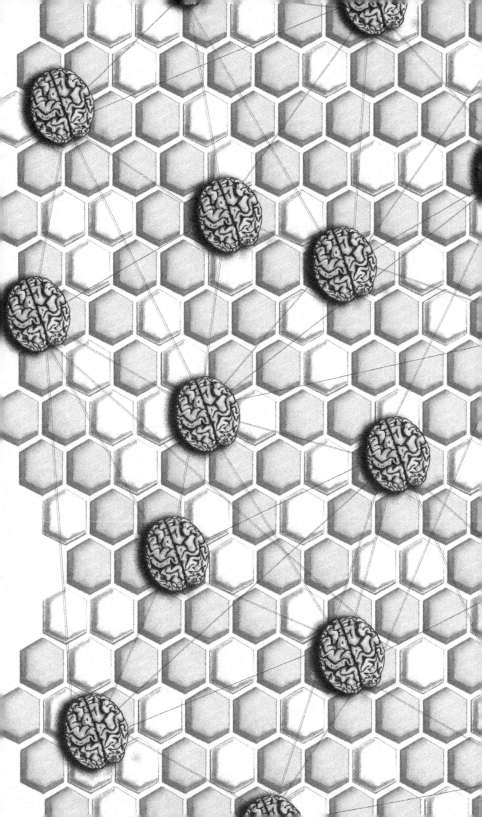

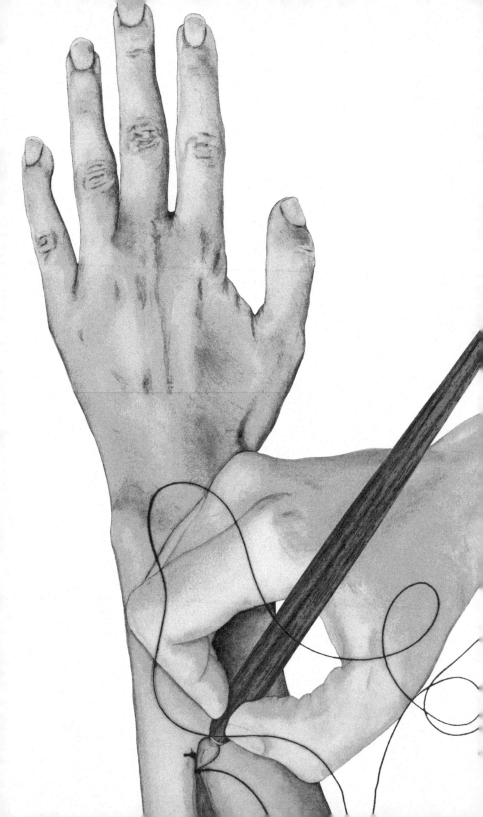

Horror Writer (I Become)

Macabre yarns birth inside my brain,
dark outcomes I take shelter in,
precious pain based on my own.

Draining my wounds onto the page
memories haunt me and I sit back
watching chunks of my existence turn into tales.

Scars and bruises combust into words
abuse and deceit, paragraphs
love and dust, devices to build up dread.

A puppeteer is all I'll ever be,
mastering endless versions of myself at play,
those who I had once been and I am no more,
those who I wish I could have been and never were,
and them, bleak-selves, who I never dared to roam.

Vomiting sorrow, grief and loss like bile
cutting my insides open with a butcher's knife
only to find out what else is there to use.

Pushing through never-ending drafts and edits,
to find an unexpected resolution, an alternative way,
for vanity and self-doubt to devour each other again.

Writing horror fiction makes me wonder
why absolution is all my pen craves
when doom is all my soul can take.

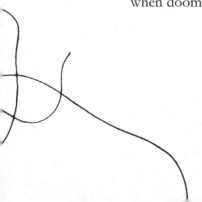

TRIGGERS

They don't realise
how their words
caress my triggers.

No matter how I illustrate
it's not control I seek
but fairness, peace, quiet.
Sympathy is all I get.

Eyes that see me
yet can't comprehend
that body language,
angry outbursts

it's all it takes
to squeeze the trigger
that sets me off.

Frozen in place, torn,
fighting my way back
to those who can't understand
flying is all I know.

'STRAYA

You speak funny,
what're ya sayin'?
You heard that wrong,
ya dreamin'.

I'm not racist but,
what's wrong with you
you fuckin' wog,
why are you here?

There's a language barrier
between you and me.
Nevermind what ya say
no one'll believe you.

You'll never work again
I'll make sure of it.
Don't care what a paper says,
you can't buy your way in.

Not one of us,
not talking like that,
not looking like that.
This is 'Straya.

NOT (A) LIST

My first love was a boy
Green Eyes was a gentle soul
with the most jealous temper.
Right after him a confident man
Brown Eyes was lust and fire,
faithful only to his own.
Third time lucky was not so,
two musicians yearned for me
yet I loved them not.
A free spirit came next
sweeping me off high, oh so high
letting me down, low, oh so low.
The Dutchman with the boy's eyes knew no better
than to hold onto me 'til he needed me no more.
It was then that I met the one
whom I gave myself the most
the one who never knew what went wrong.
And there were the ghosts
of those flickering in between.
Seventeen years it took
to find my worth
to see that I needed them
NOT.

THEY

'Why is the light still on?'
voices travel through class walls,
'It is no more,'
no other light but the sun inside my books
as I wander off hoping not to return.

'Why is the water still running?'
voices demand, patience gone.
'It is no more,'
no more waste to cleanse the likes of me
escaping down the drains while I prevail.

'Why are your eyes crossed when you're mad?'
the fire in their words branded on my skin.
'I am not'
for unlike you, I have no sense of control
cursed no matter what I say or do.

'Why are you here? You don't belong'
their eyes cry out, unable to let it go.
'I do not know,'
I wish I could just punch you in the face
but that's more trouble than you're worth.

'Why do you keep running away?
A coward is all you'll ever be'.
'Perhaps you're right,'
I am running into the unknown
yet I am not scared, but ecstatic.
A kind of brave you'll never know…

JOINT PRETENCE

'Look at you, girls, playing so well'
My father's words resonate around us until he's gone
and she pushes me into the well.

'It's a game, can't you see?'
Her mother makes her case, standing right beside him,
when they found me in our room, tied up and gagged at her feet.

'They'll never believe you, so why bother?'
My stepsister's will stronger than my own
so I take it, and I never speak, or scream, or cry out.

Because she's the youngest and I am the eldest
shy and naïve, vulnerable, that's her pretence
and I am nothing more than a loud chatterbox.
Nobody listens to me, no matter how much I say
and I retreat, writing stories of my own
and I escape, reading about lands far beyond my reach.

From fourteen to seventeen I am trapped
a shadow of the light I used to yield years before
biding my time until I turn eighteen.

But one night I can bear it no more,
scars new and old burning deep in my skin
bruises that should have never been, darkening my soul.

Way before the date and time of my birth
February finds me sneaking out of my father's place,
walking back into a life I never thought I deserved.
Ending her game, pretending no more.

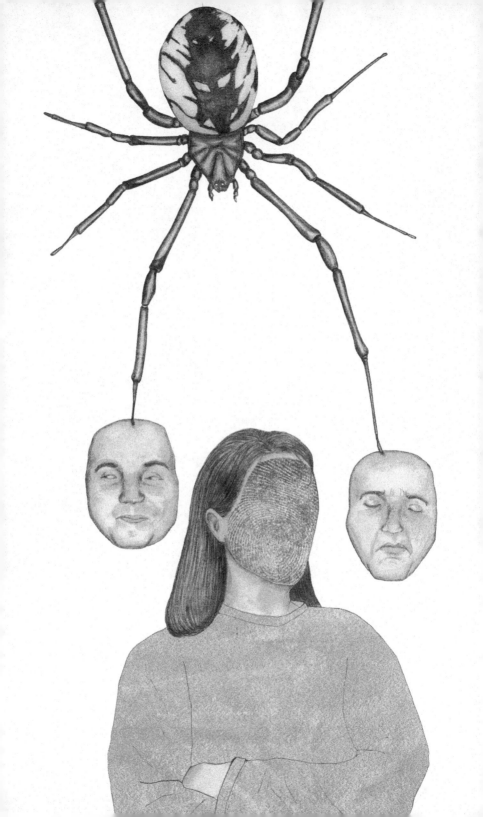

DAVID. ME. WHY

Meningitis C
is what took
my brother away
he was three years old.
Strabismus
amblyopia
scoliosis
were the gifts I bore.
My parents welcomed
a cross-eyed baby girl
with a twisted spine.
No wonder they split
before I turned five.
I didn't belong
not at home
a mere replacement
of their perfect child,
not at school
a walking birth defect
Screaming
my peer's fury unleashed.
Not a thing mattered
not what I said
not how I dressed

so I stopped trying.
I was no one
and that I became
changing cities
transferring schools
never long enough
in the one place.
Repeating
the same pattern
as I grew older.
First
moving countries
soon continents.
But no matter how far I went
her face stares at me
in the mirror.
A cross-eyed baby girl
Always unsettled
never fitting in.
Wondering why
she made it
and he didn't.

Silvia Cantón Rondoni is a Spanish-born Australian poet, writer, and visual artist who identifies as neurodivergent and LGBTIQA+. She is currently editing a poetry anthology for IFWG with the themes of hope and resilience during COVID.

Experienced editor and literary translator, Silvia runs Telltale Literary Translation from her home-office in Canberra, where she lives with her partner award-winning New Zealand writer Paul Mannering and her bulldog Patch.

Silvia Nieto is a Spanish-born illustrator and pattern designer based in the UK. Website: https://www.bysilvianieto.com/en/home-en/